KOFI KINGSTON

BY NICK GORDON

BELLWETHER MEDIA · MINNEAPOLIS, MN

Are you ready to take it to the extreme?
Torque books thrust you into the action-packed world
of sports, vehicles, mystery, and adventure. These books
may include dirt, smoke, fire, and dangerous stunts.
WARNING: read at your own risk.

Library of Congress Cataloging-in-Publication Data

Gordon, Nick.
 Kofi Kingston / by Nick Gordon.
   p. cm. -- (Torque: pro wrestling champions)
 Includes bibliographical references and index.
 Summary: "Engaging images accompany information about Kofi Kingston. The combination of
high-interest subject matter and light text is intended for students in grades 3 through 7"--Provided by
publisher.
 ISBN 978-1-60014-784-5 (hardcover : alk. paper)
 1. Kingston, Kofi, 1981---Juvenile literature. 2. Wrestlers--United States--Biography--Juvenile literature.
3. Wrestlers--Ghana--Biography--Juvenile literature. I. Title.
 GV1196.K62G67 2013
 796.812092--dc23   2011053018

This edition first published in 2013 by Bellwether Media, Inc.

Printed in the United States of America, North Mankato, MN.

A special thanks to Devin Chen, John Smolek, and David Seto for contributing images

CONTENTS

WARNING!

The wrestling moves used in this book are performed
by professionals. Do not attempt to reenact any
of the moves performed in this book.

VICTORY TIMES TWO

Kofi Kingston launched himself from the top rope. He smashed into Dolph Ziggler with a devastating Diving Crossbody. Kingston quickly made the pin. The fans went wild as Kingston celebrated. He had just won World Wrestling Entertainment's (WWE's) Intercontinental Championship for the third time!

VITAL STATS

Wrestling Name: _____ Kofi Kingston

Real Name: _____ Kofi Sarkodie-Mensah

Height: _____ 6 feet (1.8 meters)

Weight: _____ 212 pounds (96 kilograms)

Started Wrestling: _____ 2006

Finishing Move: _____ Trouble in Paradise

Suddenly, Ziggler attacked Kingston from behind. His manager demanded an instant rematch. Kingston appeared to be in trouble as Ziggler pounded on him. Ziggler was going for a big move when Kingston suddenly hit him with a Trouble in Paradise. The kick sent Ziggler to the mat for good. Kingston had won and defended his title all in one night!

7

Kofi Sarkodie-Mensah was born on August 14, 1981 in Ghana, West Africa. His family moved to Massachusetts when he was little. Young Kofi loved sports. Basketball and wrestling were his favorites.

Kofi was one of the best high school wrestlers in the state. After high school, he studied communications at Boston College. He worked for an **advertising** company after he graduated.

Kofi did not want to work in an office forever. He dreamed of being a professional wrestler. He started training and wrestling in local leagues. In 2006, he signed a **developmental contract** with WWE. He wrestled in Deep South Wrestling (DSW) as Kofi Nahaje Kingston. He claimed that he was from Jamaica.

QUICK HIT!

Shawn Michaels is one of Kofi's wrestling heroes.

SHAWN MICHAELS

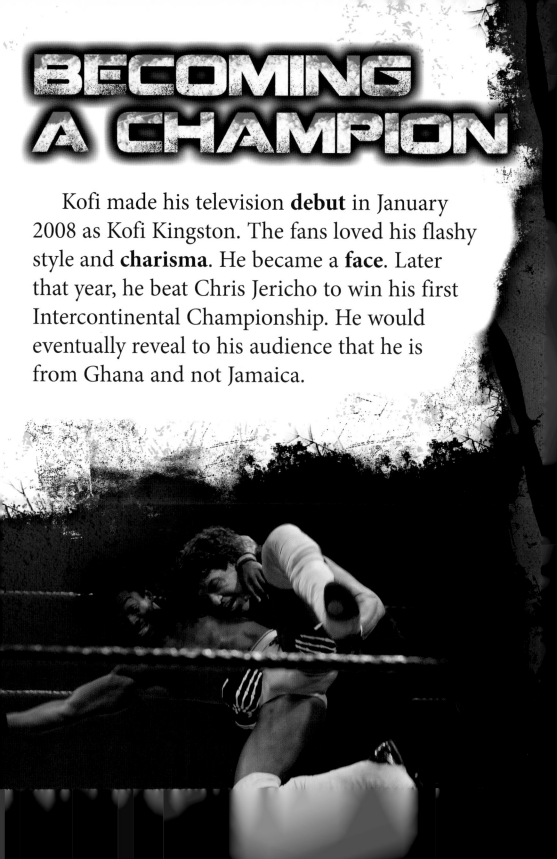

BECOMING A CHAMPION

Kofi made his television **debut** in January 2008 as Kofi Kingston. The fans loved his flashy style and **charisma**. He became a **face**. Later that year, he beat Chris Jericho to win his first Intercontinental Championship. He would eventually reveal to his audience that he is from Ghana and not Jamaica.

QUICK HIT!

Kofi was the first wrestler born in Ghana to win a WWE title.

Kingston quickly became a force in WWE. He and CM Punk teamed up to win the World Tag Team Championship in 2008. He won the WWE United States Championship in 2009 and held it for four months. In 2011, he teamed up with Evan Bourne to win the WWE Tag Team Championship. Soon after, the duo became an official tag team called Air Boom.

QUICK HIT!

Kingston's hairstyle
earned him the nickname
"The Dreadlocked Dynamo."

Kingston's high-flying **signature moves** get fans on their feet. For the Boom Drop, Kingston launches himself into the air. He crashes down on the opponent with his rear end and the back of his legs. To perform the Diving Crossbody, he climbs to the top rope and throws himself off. He lands on the opponent's chest, knocking him off his feet for the pin.

BOOM
DROP

19

Fans go wild when Kingston performs the Trouble in Paradise. For this **finishing move**, he spins toward his opponent. Then he jumps and swings one leg out to deal a vicious kick to the opponent's head. The opponent falls to the mat for an easy pin. It is yet another victory for the spirited Kofi Kingston!

GLOSSARY

advertising—the business of promoting products or services to the public

charisma—charm and personal appeal

debut—a first appearance

developmental contract—an agreement in which a wrestler signs with WWE but then wrestles in smaller leagues to gain experience and develop skills

face—a wrestler seen by fans as a hero

finishing move—a wrestling move meant to finish off an opponent so that he can be pinned

signature moves—moves that a wrestler is famous for performing

TO LEARN MORE

AT THE LIBRARY

Black, Jake. *The Ultimate Guide to WWE*. New York, N.Y.: Grosset & Dunlap, 2011.

Gordon, Nick. *Dolph Ziggler*. Minneapolis, Minn.: Bellwether Media, 2012.

Kaelberer, Angie Peterson. *Cool Pro Wrestling Facts*. Mankato, Minn.: Capstone Press, 2011.

ON THE WEB

Learning more about Kofi Kingston is as easy as 1, 2, 3.

1. Go to www.factsurfer.com.

2. Enter "Kofi Kingston" into the search box.

3. Click the "Surf" button and you will see a list of related Web sites.

With factsurfer.com, finding more information is just a click away.

INDEX